AARON RODGERS

SUPER BOWL MVP

DANIEL E. HARMON

Britannica
Educational Publishing

IN ASSOCIATION WITH

ROSEN
EDUCATIONAL SERVICES

Published in 2019 by Britannica Educational Publishing (a trademark of Encyclopædia Britannica, Inc.) in association with The Rosen Publishing Group, Inc.
29 East 21st Street, New York, NY 10010

Distributed exclusively by Rosen Publishing.
To see additional Britannica Educational Publishing titles, go to rosenpublishing.com.

First Edition

Britannica Educational Publishing
J.E. Luebering: Executive Director, Core Editorial
Andrea R. Field: Managing Editor, Compton's by Britannica

Rosen Publishing
Kathy Kuhtz Campbell: Senior Editor
Nicole Russo-Duca: Series Designer and Book Layout
Cindy Reiman: Photography Manager
Sherri Jackson: Photo Researcher

Library of Congress Cataloging-in-Publication Data

Title: Aaron Rodgers : Super Bowl MVP / Daniel E. Harmon.
Description: First Edition. | New York: Britannica Educational Publishing, in Association with Rosen Educational Services, 2019. | Series: Living legends of sports | Audience: Grades: 5–8. | Includes bibliographical references and index.
Identifiers: LCCN 2018016337| ISBN 9781538303979 (Library bound) | ISBN 9781538303962 (Paperback)
Subjects: LCSH: Rodgers, Aaron, 1983—Juvenile literature. | Quarterbacks (Football)—United States—Biography—Juvenile literature. | Football players—United States—Biography—Juvenile literature.
Classification: LCC GV939.R6235 H37 2019 | DDC 796.332092 [B] —dc23
LC record available at https://lccn.loc.gov/2018016337

Manufactured in the United States of America

CONTENTS

INTRODUCTION

Dateline: December 3, 2015. It was fourth down with time on the clock for just one play. The Green Bay Packers had the football on their own 39-yard-line, trailing the Detroit Lions 23–21. Quarterback Aaron Rodgers took the snap and rolled to his left, buying time for his receivers to race to the end zone. He then circled to his right and, with a lunging hop, flung the ball as high and far as he could. Amid the jostling, leaping melee of receivers and defenders waiting in the end zone, tight end Richard Rodgers managed to settle the ball into his chest for the winning touchdown.

A month later in a divisional playoff game against Arizona, Aaron Rodgers did it again. In the last seconds of regulation, he threw an off-balance touchdown bomb to wide receiver Jeff Janis, forcing overtime (although Arizona ultimately won the game).

National Football League (NFL) fans during the offseason watch perpetual replays of those and other fantastic connections thrown by Rodgers. If a team is in a last-second, Hail Mary pass situation, many agree Aaron Rodgers is the best man to have at quarterback.

But there is much more to Rodgers's success than a lucky arm. He enters each game well prepared to make his share of phenomenal plays. It is based not on luck but on lifelong dedication, discipline, and tireless practice. Rodgers is known for his consistent passing accuracy and low ratio of interceptions—and he constantly strives to be even better. In *Football's Greatest Stars* by Allan Maki, Rodgers states, "I want to be relentless and flawless in my decision making. I'm very driven to be the best. I think I can play more consistently."

Quarterback Aaron Rodgers of the Green Bay Packers steps back to make a pass in a game against the Detroit Lions on December 3, 2015.

CHAPTER ONE

A Pro Quarterback in the Making

Aaron Charles Rodgers was born on December 2, 1983, in Chico, California. His parents, Edward Wesley Rodgers and Darla Leigh Pittman Rodgers, had three sons: Luke, then Aaron, then Jordan.

Aaron posed with his family (*left to right*: brother, Jordan; father, Ed; mother, Darla; and grandparents, Barbara and Chuck Pittman) after being named Most Valuable Player in Super Bowl XLV.

The father, Ed Rodgers, a chiropractor by profession, played offensive guard at Chico State University (1973–76). From 1978 to 1981, he played semi-professional (semi-pro) football for the Twin City Cougars in Marysville, California. Twin City won the semi-pro national championship in 1980.

Aaron and his brothers obviously were motivated to play football by their father. But looking back, Aaron cites other qualities and examples handed down by both parents as being important to his successful career. "I am blessed that my dad is a chiropractor," he was quoted as saying in an article in the *Chiropractic Advantage*. "Getting adjusted regularly—along with practicing other good health habits that my mom helped me to establish—are all part of my goal to win in life and on the field."

The family members have said Aaron inherited his deft footwork from his mother. Aaron's mother was a dancer when she met his father.

A Three-Year-Old Armchair Quarterback

Rodgers's parents recall that by the time he was three, Aaron would watch an entire football game on television, sitting captivated and motionless. He quickly claimed for his favorite NFL team the San Francisco 49ers, propelled to championships during those years by quarterback Joe Montana.

It soon became apparent the child had physical talent as well as mental aptitude for the game. At the age of five, Aaron was tossing the ball through the center of a swinging tire. As he watched his 49ers on TV, he could understand some of the formations in which they lined up.

All three brothers were eager to play football. Their father, however, would not let them try out until they entered high school. He worried that they would be injured, acquire bad athletic habits, or simply burn out before they reached the point at which they could begin to progress in skills.

Pro Football Hall of Famer Joe Montana, quarterback of the San Francisco 49ers (1979–92), was one of Aaron's football heroes.

Chico was the family's home except for a brief period when Aaron was in middle school. During that time, the Rodgerses relocated to Oregon, where Ed attended chiropractic school. While there, although forbidden to play football, Aaron played Little League baseball. He took turns at center field, shortstop, and—not surprisingly—pitcher.

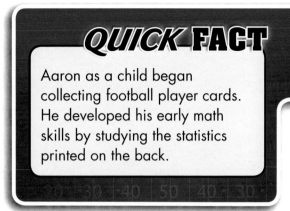

QUICK FACT

Aaron as a child began collecting football player cards. He developed his early math skills by studying the statistics printed on the back.

Beginning His Gridiron Career

Making the football team at Pleasant Valley High School in Chico, Rodgers demonstrated he was not just a competent quarterback; he had the makings of greatness. In his junior and senior seasons combined, he passed for 4,419 yards. In his final year, he completed passes for 2,303 yards, a school record. He was selected to the all-section team both years. He also was a pitcher on the Pleasant Valley baseball team.

Aaron attended Pleasant Valley High School in Chico, California. Besides being a quarterback for the Pleasant Valley Vikings, he also pitched on the school's baseball team.

Rodgers was smallish as a high school quarterback, only 5 feet 11 inches, 165 pounds. (He currently stands 6 feet 2 inches and weighs 225 pounds.) He attributes his unimpressive size as the reason no college football program offered him a scholarship out of high school. Even an excellent academic record—just short of a straight-A average and a score of 1310 on the SAT—could not compensate for his comparatively slight build.

He enrolled at Butte Community College in Oroville, California, in 2002 and began building his reputation as an outstanding quarterback. He led the team, the Roadrunners, to a number two ranking among junior colleges and the NorCal Conference title, finishing the season with a 10–1 record. His statistics were amazing: 2,408 passing yards, a 61.9-percent completion record, 28 touchdowns, and a minimal four interceptions. Meanwhile, he ran the ball for seven touchdowns.

His year at Butte proved to be an important stepping stone. University of California, Berkeley, coach Jeff Tedford, while studying

On November 20, 2004, Rodgers passed for 120 yards and a touchdown for the Cal Golden Bears, who defeated the Stanford Cardinal, 41–6.

footage of another Butte player, took notice of Rodgers's skills. Tedford watched him practice and play and was even more impressed. He offered Rodgers a scholarship to transfer to Berkeley and play for the Golden Bears. Halfway through his sophomore season at Berkeley, Rodgers earned the role of starter at quarterback.

Stardom at Cal

His statistics at the University of California, known as Cal, foretold the brand of play Rodgers eventually would exhibit in the NFL. He recorded some impressive numbers and honors. For example, during his two years as starting quarterback, he passed for 5,469 yards, completing 63.8 percent of his throws. He threw for 43 touchdowns against 13 interceptions. He also rushed for eight touchdowns. He set school records with a 150.3 passer efficiency rating and 1.95 interception rating during his college games.

As a sophomore, he passed for 2,903 yards and 19 touchdowns, suffering just five interceptions. His completion record was 61.6 percent. He began his Cal career throwing 98 passes with no interceptions. Later in the season he passed 105 times without being intercepted. In the regular season finale against Stanford, Rodgers passed for 359 yards and ran for 55—a record for a quarterback during the rivalry's 106-year history. California went to the Insight Bowl in December 2003 and defeated Virginia Tech (52–49). There, Rodgers set his personal college passing record of 394 yards.

In his junior season at Cal, Rodgers led his team to a 10–2 record. The Golden Bears rose as high as number four in the national rankings. Rodgers was named to the All-Pacific-10 first team, won several All-America honorable mentions, and was considered for the Heisman Trophy. He recorded a passing efficiency rating of 154.4. In Cal's game against the University of Southern California (USC), he completed 23 consecutive passes, tying a National Collegiate Athletic Association (NCAA) record.

In Rodgers's junior year, the Golden Bears ranked ninth in the country in the Associated Press's final poll. The season concluded with a

Rodgers attempted 42 passes but completed only 24 against the Texas Tech Red Raiders in the Pacific Life Holiday Bowl in December 2004. Cal lost the game, 31–45.

QUICK FACT

At the University of California, Rodgers majored in American Studies.

loss in the Holiday Bowl to the Texas Tech Red Raiders on December 30, 2004. Rodgers then entered the 2005 NFL Draft. He was selected in the first round by the Green Bay Packers.

Blood Brothers in Football?

Aaron is the only one of the brothers to earn national fame in football. Jordan, the youngest, played quarterback at Vanderbilt University. He signed as a free agent with the Jacksonville Jaguars in 2013. Released by the Jaguars before the season started, he later played briefly on the Tampa Bay Buccaneers' practice squad. He signed a contract to play in the Canadian Football League in 2015 with the British Columbia

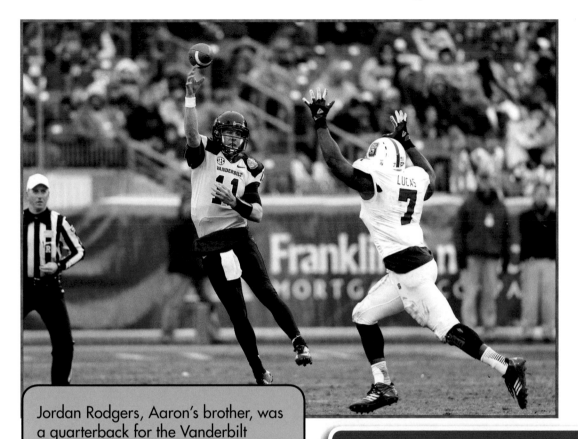

Jordan Rodgers, Aaron's brother, was a quarterback for the Vanderbilt Commodores. Here, Jordan passes the ball during the Franklin American Mortgage Music City Bowl in Nashville, Tennessee, in 2012.

QUICK FACT

Aaron Rodgers has been nicknamed "A-Rod." But the name has not really caught on for him because it was associated for years with Alex Rodriguez, a Major League Baseball player who retired in 2016.

Lions but announced his retirement from football before training began. In 2016, he took a job as college football analyst for ESPN's SEC Network.

Luke, the oldest, did not try for a football career. He is cofounder of a company that markets sports merchandise.

Rodgers Delivers at Green Bay

Aaron Rodgers was a first-round NFL Draft choice in 2005, but he was picked quite late in the round. Of the league's 32 teams, 23 bypassed him before Green Bay called his name. Draft selection is an extremely complex process. In most instances, teams first draft players to bolster their weakest positions. Although Rodgers was a leading quarterback (QB) candidate, many teams that year did not make the QB position their top priority.

Regardless, it had to have been a proud moment for Rodgers. Not only was

Rodgers, drafted 24th overall by the Green Bay Packers, holds up a Packers jersey while posing with his family and friends at the 2005 NFL Draft.

his dream of playing pro football becoming a reality; he was going to a team with one of the most honored records and reputations in the NFL.

The Legendary Packers

The Green Bay Packers are a true legacy organization in all of professional sports. The third-oldest NFL team, Green Bay owns the most season championships: 13, including four Super Bowl titles and nine pre-Super Bowl-era championships. Twenty of its players and two of its coaches are enshrined in the Pro Football Hall of Fame.

The famous Lambeau Field where the Packers play home games is named in honor of Earl "Curly" Lambeau. He played halfback and was Green Bay's first—and one of its most successful—coaches. Lambeau retired as a player in 1929 and as coach in 1949. From the late 1920s until World War II (1939–45), his Packers were championship contenders practically every year.

Statues of Earl "Curly" Lambeau (*right*) and Vince Lombardi (*left*) are displayed at the Packers' Lambeau Field. The field was dedicated in 1957 and has been renovated over the years.

15

QUICK FACT

Why are the green-and-yellow-uniformed players called the "Packers"? In 1919, a packing company in Green Bay put forth the money to start an amateur football team to compete against other community teams in Wisconsin, Minnesota, and Michigan. Two years later, the Packers, as they had become known, were accepted into the American Professional Football Association. That group in 1922 became the National Football League.

QUICK FACT

The Packer organization is the only NFL team that does not have a private owner. From virtually the beginning of the franchise, it has been a nonprofit corporation owned and supported by the citizens of Wisconsin and by Packers fans elsewhere.

After Lambeau stepped down, Green Bay languished through seven losing seasons during the 1950s. The embarrassment ceased after the organization in 1959 hired the man who would become its most famous coach, Vince Lombardi. In just his third season, Lombardi coached the Packers to an NFL championship, crushing the New York Giants, 37–0, in the title game.

Lombardi's Packers were the NFL powerhouse of the 1960s. Lombardi retired after winning the first two Super Bowls in 1967 and 1968.

Drafted to Play Backup QB

Green Bay was enjoying another long spell as an NFL powerhouse when Rodgers came to the organization. His role was cut and dried: to back up sensational QB Brett Favre, who had led the Packers to a 1997 Super Bowl victory. But there was a silver lining. Favre was on the brink of retirement. Rodgers, learning all he could from the veteran, was being groomed to succeed him.

Rodgers played in only seven games during his first three seasons with the Packers (2005–07). He developed great respect for Favre

Quarterback Brett Favre hands the ball to running back William Henderson during the Packers' Super Bowl XXXI win over the New England Patriots in January 1997. Rodgers admired Favre's playing ability and stamina.

despite being kept on the sidelines while Favre was the Packers' star. Then his role as apprentice QB drew to an abrupt end. On stormy terms with the Packers' management, Favre was traded to the New York Jets before the 2008 season began. Rodgers became the starter.

He immediately demonstrated to Packers fans and to the league that Green Bay had made a wise choice in drafting him. During the 2008 season, he passed for 4,038 yards and 28 touchdowns. For his stellar efforts, the Packers rewarded him with a $65-million contract extension spanning six years.

Pushing himself to do even better, Rodgers raised the bar the following year. He passed for 4,434 yards and 30 touchdowns. The Packers finished the 2009 season with an 11–5 record, earning a play-off berth. Rodgers's passer rating that year was 103.2, the second best in team history. He was chosen to play in the Pro Bowl.

Rodgers had given notice that he was one of the league's brightest rising stars. He was the only NFL quarterback to have thrown the ball for more than 4,000 yards in each of his first two seasons as a starter.

King of the Super Bowl

Despite Rodgers's personal prowess, few NFL analysts and fans gave the Packers high hopes as the playoffs began at the end of the 2010 season. Their regular season record was a mediocre 10–6. Rodgers had been pulled from two games because of concussions. However, he was at full strength entering the postseason.

In fact, he could hardly have looked better. Seeded sixth for the playoffs in the National Football Conference (NFC), the Packers surprisingly defeated the Philadelphia Eagles, Atlanta Falcons, and Chicago Bears—all on the road—to secure a Super Bowl berth. Rodgers's pass completion average during those three games was 71 percent.

Rodgers hands the ball off during a play against the Philadelphia Eagles in 2010. Rodgers threw for two touchdowns, and the Packers won the game, 27–20, in Philadelphia.

Rodgers raises the Lombardi Trophy after the Green Bay Packers defeated the Pittsburgh Steelers in Super Bowl XLV on February 6, 2011.

Prognosticators remained skeptical. In Super Bowl XLV, the Packers faced the Pittsburgh Steelers. A QB's experience under fire is considered vital to a team's chances for a Super Bowl victory, and Pittsburgh was led by one of the best ever. Ben Roethlisberger already had two bowl rings. Oddsmakers were confident he would bring himself and his teammates another. Rodgers had amassed amazing statistics, but he had never appeared in the big game.

It was Rodgers, though, who turned in the most masterful performance. Against the Steelers' top-rated defense, he threw for 304 yards and three touchdowns and connected on 24 of 39 pass attempts to lead Green Bay to a 31–25 victory.

Rodgers was only the fourth Super Bowl QB to pass for more than 300 yards and three touchdowns without surrendering an interception. He was chosen most valuable player (MVP) of the bowl. He also was selected as the Associated Press Male Athlete of the Year for 2011.

Rodgers's achievement surprised even people who had known of his athletic skills for years. His father told a *New York Times* reporter, "I knew Aaron had a special gift, but you never think your kid is going to wind up in the Super Bowl."

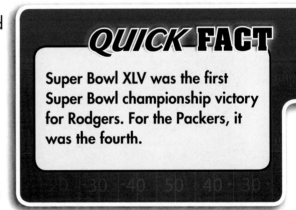

QUICK FACT

Super Bowl XLV was the first Super Bowl championship victory for Rodgers. For the Packers, it was the fourth.

Proof of Greatness

It seemed the Packers were poised to become a long-term powerhouse behind the sharp, play-by-play judgment and accurate throwing arm of Aaron Rodgers. They began the 2011 season with 13 straight victories and finished the regular season 15–1. They were clear favorites to repeat as Super Bowl champions. But the fickle fortunes of football intervened with a jolt. In their first play-off game of the postseason, the New York Giants defeated the Packers 37–20, in Green Bay.

The loss was particularly stinging to Rodgers, who was soundly outplayed by his Giants

The Packers clinched a playoff berth with their 38–35 triumph over the New York Giants in December 2011. But in the NFC divisional playoff game in January, the Packers lost to the Giants.

counterpart, Eli Manning. Rodgers completed only 26 of 46 passes. His two touchdown (TD) throws were offset by an interception. Manning, by contrast, completed 21 of 33 passes and threw for three TDs. Rodgers gave reporters a short, pointed assessment of Green Bay's performance. "We got beat by a team that played better tonight. That's the reality of this league." In February 2012, the Giants went on to defeat the New England Patriots in the Super Bowl, 21–17.

The play-off loss overshadowed what had been a landmark season for Rodgers in 2011. His biography page

QUICK FACT

Rodgers's number 12 Packers jersey today is a prize addition to sports memorabilia collections. Although Rodgers also wore number 12 when he began his football career at Pleasant Valley High School, he did not always wear that number. When he played for the Golden Bears, he wore number 8. For the Butte Roadrunners, he wore number 4.

Rodgers gives an acceptance speech after Indiana Colts quarterback Peyton Manning (*left*) presented him with the 2011 Most Valuable Player award at the NFL Honors show.

at Packers.com cites the notable statistics. Rodgers set the record for an NFL single-season passer rating, 122.5. He set team records for the most passing yardage, 4,643; most touchdown passes, 45; highest completion percentage, 68.3; and most 300-yard passing games, eight. (He tied his own record for 300-yard games three years later.) In single-game passer ratings, he set NFL records for the most 100-plus games and 110-plus games (13 and 12 games, respectively).

The rest of pro football took notice. Rodgers was chosen the NFL's MVP for the season.

Continuing to Excel—and to Disappoint

For the next five seasons, the Packers were an enigma to their fans: good enough to make the playoffs but repeatedly falling short of the Super Bowl. In 2012, they completed the regular season with an 11–5 record and won the NFC Wild Card Game against the Minnesota Vikings, then lost to the San Francisco 49ers. Rodgers performed well in both playoff games, passing for 274 and 257 yards, respectively. His contract expired that year, but there was little doubt he would be resigned as the Packers' franchise quarterback. He negotiated a $110-million, five-year contract extension.

It was the handsomest extension package in league history. Predictably, it brought with it considerable pressure from fans for Rodgers to lead the Packers back to the Super Bowl.

During the first half of the 2013 season, it appeared he just might deliver. He guided the team to a 5–2 opening record. Then, in their first game of the year against their nemesis the Chicago Bears, Rodgers suffered a broken collarbone. He missed the next six games, and the team slipped to a 7–7–1 record. He returned for the season finale, a rematch with the Bears, and got revenge with a 33–28 victory. This win propelled the Packers into the Wild Card playoffs, where they lost their first game to the San Francisco 49ers, 31–45.

Although Minnesota Viking Jared Allen sacked Rodgers during the Wild Card Game in December 2012, the Packers won, 24–10. Green Bay, however, lost to the San Francisco 49ers in the NFC divisional playoff game, 31–45.

QUICK FACT

Aaron Rodgers ranked 95th on *Forbes*'s list of the world's highest-paid athletes in 2015. He earned $11.6 million in his football salary and related income and $7.5 million for making paid endorsements.

The 2014 season looked more promising for Green Bay. They went 12–4 in the regular season and beat the Dallas Cowboys in their first playoff game. The Seattle Seahawks dashed their hopes in the NFC Championship Game, though, winning 28–25 in overtime. Although his team came up short once again, Rodgers threw for 4,381 yards, 38 touchdowns, and just 5 interceptions on the season to earn his second NFL MVP award.

In 2015, Rodgers recorded the worst passing stats of his career, finishing with a 92.7 rating. Still, he got the Packers into the playoffs. They lost 20–26 to the Arizona Cardinals in overtime in a divisional playoff game. In 2016, he looked much stronger, passing for 40 touchdowns to lead all other NFL quarterbacks. In the playoffs, Green Bay reached the NFC Championship Game but lost to Atlanta.

QUICK FACT

Pro football QBs are perpetual targets of pass-rushing defenders and, not surprisingly, often suffer a steady series of injuries. Rodgers's ailments have included a severe shoulder injury, broken collarbone, hamstring and calf injuries, and concussions.

Rodgers and the Packers endured a disappointing 2017 season after he suffered a shoulder injury against the Minnesota Vikings in the sixth game. He underwent surgery and was placed on injured reserve for two months. He returned for one game in December, a loss to the Carolina Panthers. With the team's playoff hopes gone, Rodgers was returned to the injured reserve list. Many sports commentators believe his extended absence was the main reason for the Packers missing the playoffs—their first absence in nine years.

Rodgers looks for a receiver as the Packers play the Dallas Cowboys in the NFC divisional playoff game at Lambeau Field on January 11, 2015. The Packers defeated the Cowboys, 26–21.

Clay Matthews (*left*) presents Rodgers with a replica of the heavyweight wrestling championship belt as Rodgers holds the Lombardi Trophy aloft after the Packers won Super Bowl XLV.

Cool, Confident, and Cocky

Rodgers is famous for his unshakeable confidence on the field and sidelines. "Relax," he has assured fans and reporters when the team is in a slump. His father once told a *New York Times* interviewer, "Aaron has always had this interesting combination of being really humble and extremely confident."

When he was a backup quarterback for the Packers, he amused his scout teammates by encircling his waist with an imaginary belt when they made a good play against the starting defense. It mimicked pro wrestlers strapping on the world championship belt. After becoming a starter, he celebrated touchdowns by repeating the gesture, to Packers fans' great delight.

As Rodgers stood at the podium to receive the Lombardi Trophy after winning Super Bowl XLV in 2011, teammate Clay Matthews slyly presented him with another trophy: a replica of the heavyweight wrestling championship belt. Rodgers has been honored similarly at other public events.

CHAPTER FOUR

Aaron Rodgers in Street Clothes

NFL television viewers were treated to an insurance commercial with a hilarious twist at the beginning of the 2017 season. Rodgers and his pet dog (a canine actor named Rigsbee) are surveying with an agent damage caused by a drone that has crashed into his truck windshield. According to the story line, Rodgers and Rigsbee have had

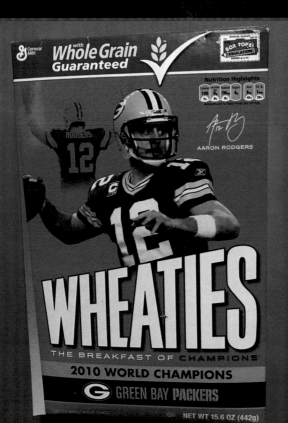

Aaron Rodgers was featured on the cereal box for Wheaties that also honored the 2010 World Champion Packers team.

wonderful adventures in the truck for seven years, and the vehicle never has been blemished. Flashback video clips show the pair in some of their cutest moments while the pop song "Believe It or Not" plays in the background. The commercial concludes with Packer teammate Clay Matthews arriving on the scene apologetically holding his drone control, to be growled at by a vindictive Rigsbee.

Those kinds of cleverly produced off-the-field appearances have endeared Rodgers to millions of Americans who care nothing for the Green Bay Packers. Rodgers also has endorsed Pizza Hut, Wheaties, and many regional brands.

Sorting Private Affairs from Public Interest

Rodgers frequently grants interviews, not just to sports media but also to entertainment reporters. He is respected for his thoughtful, informative responses, often laced with humor. On certain topics, though, he is guarded. He does not complain strongly about the intrusions imposed on celebrities by a curious press. He stands his ground, though, when he believes comments about personal matters would be inappropriate.

Rodgers has never married. He reportedly was engaged to a high school friend, but he has declined to discuss the matter. He dated Olivia Munn, an actress, for three years until 2017. The reason for their breakup seemed linked to the high public profiles each of them have.

At the beginning of 2018, the entertainment media confirmed that he was dating Danica Patrick. Patrick is a NASCAR driver and author (and Chicago Bears fan).

Rodgers's family in 2016 confirmed that their relationship with their famous son had been strained for some time. His parents did not attend any of the Packers games that year, and Aaron reportedly was not speaking to his family. Details of the reason for the tension have not been clear. Entertainment commentators speculate that his parents strongly disapproved when he began dating Olivia Munn in 2014, which was said to have deeply angered the celebrity quarterback. Another trigger

Rodgers and his girlfriend, racing driver Danica Patrick (*left*), appeared together before the Daytona 500 race at Daytona International Speedway in 2018.

may relate to competitive rivalries between Aaron and his brothers. Some observers attribute it simply to "the price of fame."

Still Rooted in California

Del Mar is a beach city that lies along the Pacific coast in California. Rodgers owns a home in Del Mar, one in Los Angeles, and another in Suamico, Wisconsin.

Rodgers lives in Suamico, Wisconsin, a suburb about 10 miles from Green Bay. During the offseason, though, he's most likely to be seen in his home state. He owns a home in Del Mar, California, a ritzy oceanfront community. But he spends most of his time at his third home in Los Angeles.

Reporter Mina Kimes of *ESPN: The Magazine* says that Rodgers is typical of a small-town native who has become awed by the metropolis. "He likes it all: the live music, the organic grocery stores, the expectation that he can walk around without being stalked by middle-aged men with Sharpies asking him to sign memorabilia they'll later sell on eBay."

Rodgers relishes being in Los Angeles, where he does not have to be constantly mindful of his celebrity status. He explained to Kimes in an interview that people in Los Angeles "see a lot more famous and recognizable people than me every day."

QUICK FACT

Rodgers's extravagant beach community estate in Del Mar reflects the interests of its owner. It features not only a pool, full gym, basketball court, and gaming room, but a football field (actual dimensions not reported).

A Passion for Music

Rodgers began teaching himself to play guitar and occasionally jams with teammates. In a 2012 interview with Vic Ketchman at Packers.com, he said he learned to play "a handful of songs" and became "decent at reading and interpreting music. I like to hear something and figure out what the chord progression is." Eventually, he signed up for guitar lessons in Green Bay.

He has told interviewers he enjoys various styles of music but especially the work of singer-songwriters. The first song he tried to learn was "Forever" by Ben Harper.

As part of his itsAaron.com website series, Rodgers once surprised a 13-year-old to collaborate in composing and recording a song together onstage at the Pabst Theater in

QUICK FACT

In 2011, Rodgers started a record label in California. Suspended Sunrise Recordings was intended to help promote the careers of alternative rock bands. The first group he signed, called The Make, was from Chico, his hometown.

Milwaukee. The girl, who loves to sing, has the condition spina bifida. ItsAaron.com profiles Wisconsinites who have benefited from the efforts of nonprofit organizations. In this instance, the charity was IndependenceFirst, which helps children who have disabilities.

Rodgers also enjoys a variety of sports and recreational activities and is an avid golfer. Noted as a scratch golfer, he participates in a number of celebrity and charity tournaments such as the Vince Lombardi Golf Classic.

Challenging Grim Opponents Off the Field

In addition to itsAaron.com, Rodgers has supported other humanitarian programs in various ways. Based in Milwaukee, Midwest Athletes Against Childhood Cancer (the MACC Fund; https://www.maccfund .org) has been working to end childhood cancer for more than 40 years. The MACC Fund finances scientific research and develops novel treatments. In 2015, Rodgers won a *Celebrity Jeopardy* episode and designated the fund to receive the $50,000 award.

Rodgers also took a deep interest in Raise Hope for Congo. The initiative was an outreach of the Enough Project (https://enoughproject .org), which works to stop massive atrocities in some of the most violent parts of Africa.

The Packers participated in the NFL's "My Cause, My Cleats" project in a game against Tampa Bay in December 2017. Although he did not play in the game because of an injury, Rodgers wore shoes supporting the Special Olympics (https://www.specialolympics.org).

Rodgers enjoys playing golf. Here, he is seen at the AT&T Pebble Beach National Pro-Am tournament after almost making a hole-in-one at the seventh hole, in February 2012.

Rodgers poses with a child from the Make-A-Wish Foundation before a game at Lambeau Field in 2014. Rodgers supports many humanitarian efforts and often helps to make young fans' lifelong wishes come true.

Rodgers tweeted that the Special Olympics "honors some incredible athletes" and is an inspiration to him personally.

Attached to Green Bay

Rogers has said he hopes to complete his professional football career in Green Bay. Although it is a comparatively small NFL city, having a population of fewer than 100,000, the Packers organization is fiscally healthy and enjoys staunch support from its fans.

Much of the reason for that at this point in franchise history is Aaron Rodgers. During the past decade, he has led the team repeatedly to glory. Much of the reason for the success of his efforts is his lifelong work ethic. Always a keen student of the game, he relentlessly seeks to improve himself. His hard work and discipline inspire teammates, as does his unique aura of leadership even while coping with injuries and weathering slumps in performance.

TIMELINE

1983: Aaron Charles Rodgers is born on December 2 in Chico, California.

1988: By age five, Aaron is throwing a football accurately and studying formations used by the San Francisco 49ers in their televised games.

2000–2001: In his junior and senior seasons as quarterback at Pleasant Valley High School in Chico, Rodgers sets passing records and is named to the all-section team both years.

2002: Rodgers enrolls at Butte Community College in Oroville and plays one season as quarterback. He leads the team to a 10–1 record and the NorCal Conference championship and establishes himself as an exceptionally accurate passer.

2003: Rodgers receives a scholarship to the University of California at Berkeley. During his two years at the helm of the football offense, he sets school records for passer efficiency and leads the Golden Bears to two postseason bowl appearances. In his final year as a junior, he is mentioned as a possible All-America and Heisman Trophy candidate.

2005: The Green Bay Packers select Rodgers in the first round of the NFL Draft.

2008: Rodgers becomes Green Bay's starting quarterback after the departure of Brett Favre.

2011: The Packers win Super Bowl XLV despite having a mediocre 2010 regular season. Rodgers is selected Associated Press Male Athlete of the Year and most valuable NFL player for the 2011 season.

2011: The Packers complete a 15–1 regular season and seem poised to return to the Super Bowl but lose their first playoff game.

2012: Rodgers gets a five-year, $110-million contract extension.

2013–16: The Green Bay Packers manage to make the playoffs each year but do not reach the Super Bowl.

2014: Rodgers is named the NFL's most valuable player of the season for the second time.

2017: Rodgers misses most of the season after suffering a severe shoulder injury. After returning for one game in December, he again is placed on the injured reserve roster.

OTHER LIVING LEGENDS OF FOOTBALL

Joe Montana (1956–) is a four-time Super Bowl champion and three-time Super Bowl MVP. He was a Hall of Fame quarterback for the San Francisco 49ers from 1979–1992 and the Kansas City Chiefs from 1993–1994. In college, he led the University of Notre Dame to a national championship in 1977.

Tom Brady (1977–) has been the quarterback for the New England Patriots since 2000. He has won the NFL Most Valuable Player and NFL Comeback Player of the Year awards. Brady has guided the Patriots to five Super Bowl wins, earning game MVP in four of those wins. He has also been selected for the Pro Bowl 12 times.

Drew Brees (1979–) led the New Orleans Saints to the franchise's first Super Bowl berth, a victory over the Indianapolis Colts in Super Bowl XLIV. In 2011, Brees broke Dan Marino's single-season passing yardage record, finishing the season with 5,476 yards through the air. He broke his own league record for completion percentage, 71.2, established an all-time NFL mark by passing for more than 300 yards in 13 games, and threw a personal-best 46 touchdown passes. He broke Johnny Unitas's record for most consecutive games with a touchdown pass when he threw for a score in his 48th straight game in 2012. In 2013, Brees threw for 5,162 yards to notch his fourth career 5,000-yard season.

Philip Rivers (1981–) stands unique among the small circle of extraordinary NFL quarterbacks whose year-to-year achievements have proven them to be the best of the best of the 21st century. He has been the team's starting QB all but the first two years of his career. Since becoming a starter, he has led the Los Angeles Chargers into the playoffs five times. Rivers has been a Pro Bowl pick six times. In 2017, he passed for 4,515 yards, throwing 28 touchdown passes with 10 interceptions.

Russell Wilson (1988–) was chosen by the Seattle Seahawks in the third round of the NFL Draft in 2012. He soon proved to be a sterling pick. He led the Seahawks to a stunning 43–8 victory over the Denver Broncos in Super Bowl XLVIII in 2014. A former minor league baseball player, he has expressed an interest in returning to that game. His baseball rights were acquired by the New York Yankees in February 2018.

Harrison Smith (1989–) is generally regarded as one of the best safeties in the NFL. The Notre Dame product was drafted in the first round in 2012 by the Minnesota Vikings. He is especially noted for his high ratios of tackles—including quarterback sacks and ball carrier stops in the opponents' backfield. As team captain in his last season at Notre Dame, he made 90 tackles. In his rookie season at Minnesota, he was involved in 104 tackles and made three interceptions, returning two of them for touchdowns. Smith was named to the 2016, 2017, and 2018 Pro Bowls.

Julio Jones (1989–) is one of the NFL's most exciting wide receivers and was a record-setting player at the University of Alabama when he was chosen by the Atlanta Falcons in the first round of the 2011 NFL Draft. During the Falcons' 2016 Super Bowl loss, he made a fantastic catch late in the game, which placed the Falcons in what seemed to be a game-winning position. However, Atlanta failed to score and went on to lose the bowl to New England. Jones has been a Pro Bowl selection five times. He has fumbled the ball only eight times in his pro career, with no fumbles in his 2016 and 2017 seasons.

Tyron Smith (1990–) is an offensive lineman. The Dallas Cowboys chose left tackle Tyron Smith in 2011 and have not regretted the decision. Smith was a standout lineman at Rancho Verde High School in California and at the University of Southern California. Drafted by Dallas after his junior season, he started at right offensive tackle in his first Cowboys season, then switched to the left ("blind") side. The fierce quarterback protector and run blocker has made the Pro Bowl team for five consecutive years.

Luke Kuechly (1991–) greatly impressed pro scouts as a linebacker at Boston College where he set Atlantic Coast Conference and school records for number of tackles, tackles for lost yardage, sacks, fumble recoveries, forced fumbles, and pass interceptions. He entered the NFL Draft following his junior season and was picked by the Carolina Panthers in the first round in 2012. As a pro, he has become known for his uncommon instincts for where the ball is going, field of vision, brute strength, and speed.

GLOSSARY

aptitude A natural ability to do something or to learn something.

atrocity A shockingly bad or cruel act, object, or situation.

aura A special quality or feeling that seems to come from a person, place, or thing.

calf Muscular back quadrant of the lower leg.

chiropractor Licensed medical professional who mainly treats skeletal and muscular problems.

concussion Injury to the brain caused by a severe blow to the head.

fiscally Pertaining to financial matters.

formations Different patterns in which offensive and defensive players line up at the beginning of each play.

franchise A team that is a member of a professional sports league.

franchise quarterback Star quarterback around whom an NFL organization believes it can build a successful franchise.

gridiron Football field.

Hail Mary pass A long forward pass thrown into or near the end zone in a last-ditch effort to score as time runs out.

hamstring Tendon or muscle at the back of the knee or thigh.

injured reserve List of disabled players who are members of a team but are not listed on the official roster.

Lombardi Trophy Named after former NFL player and coach Vince Lombardi, the Lombardi Trophy is the prize that an NFL team receives for winning the Super Bowl.

melee A confusing struggle for position on a playing field.

memorabilia Things of the past that are treasured collector's items to people with certain interests.

nemesis One who inflicts punishment in return for an injury or offense.

NFL Draft An annual event in which NFL teams select college football players to play for them.

passer rating Statistical measure of a quarterback's passing performance based on completions, touchdowns, yardage, and interceptions.

physique The form of a person's bodily structure.

Pro Bowl The NFL's version of an all-star game in which the players are voted on by coaches, fans, and their peers.

prognosticator One who predicts future events or developments.

scout teammates Nonstarting players who emulate the anticipated play of the upcoming opponent team during practice against the starting squad.

scratch golfer An accomplished amateur player who usually shoots par or lower.

spina bifida A debilitating back disorder, typically caused by a birth defect.

Super Bowl The annual championship game in the NFL between the top teams from the American Football Conference and the National Football Conference.

Wild Card An NFL team that makes the playoffs despite not winning a divisional conference title.

Books

Aretha, David. *Aaron Rodgers: Champion Football Star*. New York, NY: Enslow Publishing, 2018.

Doeden, Matt. *The Super Bowl: Chasing Football Immortality*. Minneapolis, MN: Millbrook Press, 2018.

Gilbert, Sara. *The Story of the Green Bay Packers*. Mankato, MN: Creative Education, 2014.

Howell, Brian. *Green Bay Packers*. Mankato, MN: Childs World, 2016.

Lyon, Drew. *A Superfan's Guide to Pro Football Teams*. North Mankato, MN: Capstone Press, 2018.

Maki, Allan. *Football's Greatest Stars*. Buffalo, NY: Firefly Books Ltd., 2013.

Morey, Allan. *The Green Bay Packers Story*. Minneapolis, MN: Bellwether Media, 2017.

Myers, Dan. *Green Bay Packers*. Minneapolis, MN: SportsZone, 2017.

Nagelhout, Ryan. *Aaron Rodgers*. New York, NY: Gareth Stevens Publishing, 2017.

Rivkin, Jennifer. *Gridiron Greats: Heroes of Football*. New York, NY: Crabtree Publishing, 2016.

Robinson, Tom. *Today's 12 Hottest NFL Superstars*. North Mankato, MN: 12-Story Library, 2015.

Scheff, Matt. *Stunning NFL Upsets: 12 Shockers from NFL History*. North Mankato, MN: 12-Story Library, 2016.

Websites

Green Bay Packers Kids Club
http://www.packers.com/fan-zone/kids-club.html

itsAaron.com
https://www.youtube.com/user/itsaaroncom

National Football League
https://www.nfl.com

Official Website of the Green Bay Packers
http://www.packers.com